Man After Marriage

Rakesh Singh

ISBN: **978-93-5635-780-8**

DEDICATION

To every man who smiles in public and breaks in silence.

To every husband who is called *changed*.

To every son who is expected to understand everyone—but is never understood.

This book is for you

Table of Contents

Prologue: The Wedding Mandap and the Silent Promise

The lights are bright. The music is loud. Relatives are laughing.

The groom sits on the stage, smiling.

Everyone sees happiness.

No one sees fear.

As the rituals continue, elders bless him: *Now you are responsible.*

Responsible—for whom?

For everyone.

That night, when the room finally becomes quiet, a man lies awake next to a stranger who is now his wife. He makes a promise without words:

I will handle everything. I won't let anyone suffer because of me.

That promise becomes his burden.

Author's Note

This book is not against women.

This book is not against families.

This book is against silence.

Indian men are raised to endure, not express. They are taught responsibility, not emotional honesty. After marriage, they stand at the most dangerous emotional junction of life—between parents who raised them and a wife who depends on them.

Most men fail not because they are weak, but because they are unheard.

This book is a voice.

1 **Before Marriage – The Protected Son**

Before marriage, life doesn't feel light.

It *is* light.

Not because you have no problems—but because someone else is carrying them for you.

In an Indian joint family, especially as a younger son, you grow up wrapped in invisible protection. You don't see it. You don't acknowledge it. You don't even realize it exists.

Your parents worry, yes—but not about *you*. They worry about your future in an abstract way, not in monthly EMIs, grocery lists, or medical bills.

Your elder brother takes the weight without announcing it.

Your sister-in-law manages the house without reminding you.

You live inside a system that runs smoothly, and you assume life itself is smooth.

No one tells you:

This ease is borrowed.

The Comfort You Never Questioned

You wake up and tea is ready.

You come home and food is served.

Electricity bill? Paid.

Groceries? Stocked.

Medical emergency? Handled.

You never sit down with a calculator.

You never check your bank balance before stepping out.

Not because you don’t earn—but because no one makes you feel the weight of earning.

You spend ten to fifteen thousand rupees a month on yourself.

Clothes.

Shoes.

Perfume.

Haircuts.

Gym.

Not out of greed.

Out of innocence.

Because no one ever told you that money also carries stress.

Treated Like a Child, Loved Like One

Your elder brother looks at you and still sees the younger version of you.

The one who doesn't need to be burdened.

The one who should enjoy life.

Your sister-in-law scolds you like a mother and feeds you like one.

You feel independent.

But you are actually protected.

And protection, when it lasts too long, becomes a blindfold.

The Illusion of Strength

You believe you are strong.

You believe you are capable.

And you *are*—but only in theory.

Because strength that is never tested is only confidence.

You have never managed a house.

Never planned expenses beyond your own comfort.

Never felt the pressure of choosing between need and desire.

Life hasn't asked you hard questions yet.

So you assume you already know the answers.

The Dangerous Sentence: 'You'll Manage'

Relatives say it casually:

"He's smart. He'll manage after marriage."

That sentence sounds like praise.

But it is actually abandonment wrapped in optimism.

No one teaches you *how* to manage.

They just assume you will.

The Day Before Marriage

The night before marriage, you are excited.

You are nervous.

But you are not afraid.

Because you think marriage is an *addition*.

A partner.

Love.

Companionship.

You don't realize marriage is also a *transfer of weight*.

From others' shoulders to yours.

What You Didn't Know Then

You didn't know that after marriage:

- Spending money would come with guilt
- Asking for help would feel like weakness
- Silence would become your default response
- Responsibility would arrive without warning

You didn't know because no one told you.

And because society believes men don't need preparation—only pressure.

Looking Back

When you look back now, you don't feel angry.

You feel emotional.

Because you realize:

They didn't spoil you.

They *shielded* you.

Out of love.

And love, sometimes, delays growth.

Before marriage, you were not careless.

You were cared for.

Before marriage, you were not irresponsible.

You were *protected.*

And protection is beautiful—

Until the day it is taken away without warning.

You Were Loved Without Conditions

Before marriage, love was simple.

You didn't have to earn it. You didn't have to prove anything daily. You didn't have to explain your exhaustion.

You could come home tired, angry, silent—and still be accepted.

No one measured your worth by your monthly income. No one questioned your masculinity during your weakest moments. No one asked, "What are you bringing to the table?"

You were the table.

Even on days you contributed nothing.

And that kind of love does something dangerous.

It makes you comfortable.

2 Invisible Sacrifices – The Emotional Journey of a Man

There is a kind of pain a man carries that no one sees.

No scars.
No bruises.
No limping.

Just silent pressure in the chest.
A tightening around the heart.
A sense that you are holding on to something heavy, but you don't know why.

Every man sacrifices.
But most of those sacrifices are invisible.

They aren't applauded.
They aren't acknowledged.
They aren't even understood — sometimes not even by himself.

The Weight You Weren't Prepared For

Before you married, you thought you knew stress.

Bills? Manageable.
Deadlines? Scary but solvable.
Pressure? Temporary.

But nothing prepares a man for the quiet demands of life — the ones that don't make noise, don't announce themselves, and don't come with instructions.

It's not the loud crisis that crushes you.
It's the quiet moments — the ones when no one is watching

Scene — 9 PM, Living Room

His wife sleeping.
The baby crying.
Bills stacked on the side table like small towers of guilt.
He stands there.
He has no words.
Just a trembling pause.

He whispers to no one:

"How long do I have to keep doing this?"
(No answer comes.)

That silence — that is sacrifice

The Mother Who Laughed, Then Cried

Mothers see what others don't.

When you were a child, she protected you.
When you became a man, she worried without saying a word.

One day, she sat across from you and said:

"My son, life isn't easy… but you will find your way."

But in her eyes — that flicker of fear — it wasn't hope. It was concern she couldn't fix anymore.

You smiled, thinking she was strong.

Later, in the kitchen, alone… she cried.

Not loud. Not broken. Just quiet tears.

That was her sacrifice — letting you walk into fire without holding your hand.

The Sacrifice You Call "Normal"

You wake up early.
Work hard.
Ignore pain.
Lie to yourself that sleep will fix it.

You tell friends:

"It's nothing. Just tired."

But in your heart, sleep doesn't fix fear.
It only delays it.

Fear that:

you're not enough

you're failing silently

your best isn't good enough

love doesn't cover bills, dreams, or responsibilities

You don't say it.
You don't scream it.
You just carry it.

That is the invisible weight of a man

The Marriage Conversations No One Talks About

Real-life doesn't come with soft dialogues.

Some night:

Wife:
"Are you okay?"

Him (half-smile):
"Just tired."

Wife:

"You always say that."

That's when reality hits:

You're not "just tired."
You're weighed down by the cost of love you can't adequately pay yet.

She feels it.
You feel it.
But neither says it.

You Don't Lose Sleep, You Lose Parts of Yourself

You don't know when it happened.

But somewhere between bills, late nights, kids, arguments, and silent dinners — you lost pieces of who you were.

You don't laugh as freely.
You don't dream as wildly.
You don't dare to hope as recklessly.

Because every dream hurts when reality keeps tapping your shoulder.

You think:

"If I stop sacrificing, everything collapses."

So you never stop.

Never rest.
Never slow down.
Never confess exhaustion.

That is emotional sacrifice — survival without applause.

The Inner Conversation No One Hears

In the middle of night, when the world sleeps, you hear it most clearly.

Your inner voice whispers:

“Are you enough?”

And your heart fights to answer:

“I’m trying.”

Not confident.
Not certain.
Just trying.

That is a battle no one sees.

No one hears.
No one applauds.

But it warps you.
It shapes you.
It builds you quietly.

The Guilt You Wear Like a Second Skin

You're a provider, protector, dreamer, builder — but shame sits quietly behind all those roles.

You feel guilty when you:

Can't give more money

Can't give more time

Can't explain your tension

Can't balance expectations

So you bury it.

Deep.
Very deep.

So deep that it becomes part of who you think you are.

Men Don't Cry — They Go Silent

You were told:

A man doesn't cry.

So you compress emotion.

Not explosive.
Not vocal.
Just quiet.

Inside, it stacks — brick by invisible brick — until you barely recognize the person standing in the mirror.

You don't cry.
You go silent.

And silence is the heaviest burden of all.

Invisible Sacrifice Is Love With No Celebration

You love, but love doesn't come with fireworks.

You sacrifice, but sacrifices don't get trophies.

You give, and sometimes it feels like you receive nothing back.

You think:

"Is it worth it?"

Then you see your child's sleep-wrinkled smile, or hear "I love you" in soft voice at night, and think…

Maybe this is love —
Not triumphant…

Not loud…
But undeniably real.

That is emotional sacrifice

You Don't Need Applause. You Need Recognition

Not praise.
Not applause.
Not validation.

Just recognition.

Just once.

Someone to say:

"I see you."

That's all.

No grandeur.
No show.

Just truth.

And when someone finally says it?

It hurts — but it heals.

Invisible Sacrifices Never End — They Evolve

Marriage doesn't teach you how to sacrifice.
It reveals what it demands:

Not that you change.
But that you adapt without complaining.

You learn that:

Love isn't always comfortable

Support isn't always visible

Strength isn't always loud

Being a man isn't always appreciated

But you keep going anyway.

Because love — even invisible — is still worth the pain

The Quiet Victory of a Man's Heart

The greatest victory isn't wealth.
It isn't praise.
It isn't recognition.

It's this:

Continuing when you think you have nothing left.

That is emotional sacrifice.
That is quiet courage.
That is the invisible journey of a man

Reflection — Don't Just Read This. Feel It

If you're a man reading this:

Pause.

Slow down.

Ask yourself:

"What am I silently carrying right now?"

Because every invisible burden has a cost — and until you name it, you cannot release it.

Your sacrifice is real.
Your journey is hard.
Your pain is valid.

And most importantly:

You are not alone — even if it feels that way

3 Between Wife and Parents – A Story Every Man Will Understand

There are two forces in a man's life that pull him in opposite directions — love and loyalty.
Not rivals. Just equally powerful.

And once marriage begins, a strange new war begins quietly inside him.

This chapter isn't about being right or choosing sides.
It's about what it feels like to be torn — not by obvious battles, but by invisible pressures that sharpen over time… until a man barely recognizes himself.

The Invisible Tug-of-War Begins

Before marriage, family meant safety.
After marriage, it meant responsibility.

Now every call from your mother doesn't just bring warmth — it brings questions:

"Is everything okay?"

"Are you eating properly?"

"When will you visit?"

And every time your wife looks at you with tired eyes, you hear:

"I need help here."

"Can you be present?"

"Why are you quiet again?"

You are not just a son anymore.
You are now a husband — and that changes everything.

Each Word Becomes a Weight You Carry

Words from your parents don't feel heavy.

Words from your wife don't either — at first.

But as days pass, every sentence begins to echo with expectation.

Scene — Dinner Table

Father:
“Why don’t you call more often? Your mother worries.”

Him (trying to stay calm):
“Dad, it’s been a long day. I’ll call later.”

Wife (softly, under her breath):
“We never have dinner together anymore because you’re always working late.”

No explosions.
No yelling.

Just two truths — and one man caught in between.

Parents See You as Their Son — Always

Your mother still remembers you as the boy who needed comfort, warmth, protection.

She forgets — or doesn’t fully realize — that you’re no longer living in her house, under her care.

She calls at 8 PM with:

“Have you eaten? Eat properly. Don’t skip dinner.”

She doesn’t mean harm.
She means love.

But in your wife’s house — that phone call means:

You were eating late again.

You didn't eat together.
You're distant.

And suddenly, simple love becomes complicated pain.

Wife Wants Time — Parents Want Tradition

Your wife wants:

Emotional presence

Weekend connection

A partner who listens

Your parents want:

Respect

Frequency of calls

Presence during festivals and family time

Sometimes both want exactly the same thing from different grips.

And you — the man — are somewhere in the middle… holding every expectation in your chest like a hot stone.

The Unspoken Conversation Inside Your Head

There's a moment every man knows but cannot verbalize:

I love my wife.
I respect my parents.
Why does loving both feel like betraying one?

You replay conversations in your head:

Why didn't she understand I was tired?
Why did they call again during our dinner?
Why does every answer feel wrong?

And no matter what you choose, part of you feels guilty.

That's the silent suffering.

The Night You Realized You Couldn't Please Everyone

Scene — Living Room, Late Night

Your wife is asleep.
Your phone lights up.

Mother (text):
"Please come home this weekend. We miss you."

You don't want to disturb your wife.
But you also don't want to worry your mother.

Your inner voice whispers:

You can't please everyone.

But your heart screams:

Try anyway.

So you text:

"Sure, we'll come."

And you know:

You just promised something you won't enjoy… but feel obligated to keep.

That's sacrifice — not with pride, but with pain.

Guilt — The Silent Companion

Guilt doesn't shout.
It whispers.

It whispers when:

You spent too much time at work.

You didn't call your parents today.

You couldn't talk with your wife about her day.

You missed your mother's voice on the phone.

You forgot an important date at home.

Guilt sits beside you like an uninvited guest that never leaves.

It doesn't yell.
It just waits.

Sometimes Silence Hurts More Than Words

Arguments don't always happen with explosions.

Sometimes they happen with silence.

Scene — After Dinner

Wife:
"You didn't tell me your mother was sick."

Him:
"I didn't want to worry you."

Wife:
"So you worry her… but not me?"

No shouting.
Just pain.

And you're left thinking:

I didn't lose either. I just couldn't balance both.

That's the pain most men never voice.

Expectations Unspoken Are the Sharpest Blades

Parents expect:
Respect. Tradition. Frequent visits.

Wife expects:
Presence. Emotional investment. Partnership.

No one says these things openly all the time — but both feel them deeply.

And you are the bridge.

Caught between:

"Please be with us."

"Please be here with me."

You stand there — unarmed.

Love Isn't Enough — Understanding Is

Love is beautiful, but it doesn't erase conflict.

What every man needs — isn't just:

Love

Respect

Support

But understanding.

Not just saying:

"I love you."

But:

"I see you trying."

That's rare.
That's human.
That heals.

When "Choosing" Feels Like Betrayal

Life doesn't always give clear choices.

Sometimes it gives:

You — pulled two ways

Love — from both sides

Expectations — from all directions

And no instructions

So every decision feels like:

"Am I betraying someone I love?"

And the answer never feels clean.

Because love isn't always fair — but it is always demanding.

Real Pain Isn't Loud — It's Persistent

Real pain isn't screaming.

It's:

Being tired but pretending strength

Being silent but thinking deeply

Being present physically but absent emotionally

Carrying two homes' expectations on one heart

That's not drama.

That's reality.

And every man lives it — quietly — every day.

The Moment You Stop Blaming Yourself

One day — silently — you realize something:

You're not wrong.
You're not failing.
You're trying your hardest with love on both sides.

You realize:

Love doesn't demand perfection.
Love demands effort.

And that effort — even if imperfect — is enough.

The Real Victory Is Balance — Not Perfection

There is no perfect solution.
There is only:

Communication

Patience

Empathy

Honest conversation

Understanding that everyone has feelings

The moment you accept balance — not perfection — is the moment you breathe again.

This Story Is Not Just Yours — It's Every Man's

You are not alone in this struggle.

Every man who loves deeply —
Every son who respects his parents —
Every husband who wants to be a partner —
Feels this tension.

You don't have to choose sides.
You just have to learn how to hold space for both.

And that…
is the silent strength of a man.

4 “You Have Changed After Marriage” – The Painful Accusation.

There are sentences that hit harder than insults.

Not because they are loud.
But because they feel true, even when you don’t want them to be.

One of them is this:

“You have changed after marriage.”

It’s not shouted.
It’s not dramatic.
It’s often said casually — during a phone call, an argument, or a tired conversation.

But once spoken, it never leaves.

It sits inside you.
It echoes.
It questions everything you are becoming.

Who Says It — And Why It Hurts More

Your parents say it.

Your friends say it.

Sometimes, even your wife says it — indirectly.

And every time, it lands differently.

From parents, it sounds like disappointment.
From friends, it sounds like distance.
From your wife, it sounds like confusion.

But to you, it sounds like:

"You are no longer enough for us."

And that hurts — deeply.

The Day You Heard It the First Time

Scene — Phone Call With Mother

Mother:
"You don't call like before."

Him:
"I've been busy, Ma."

Mother (after a pause):
"You have changed after marriage."

Silence.

You want to explain.
You want to say a hundred things.

But all you manage is:

"Life is different now."

You hang up.

And suddenly, the room feels smaller

What They Don't See

They don't see:

You waking up earlier than before

You sleeping later than before

You worrying more than before

You carrying responsibilities no one prepared you for

They remember the version of you that had less weight.

You are still the same man.

But now, you are carrying more life on your shoulders.

Change Is Not Always Choice — Sometimes It's Survival

You didn't change because you wanted to.

You changed because:

Bills arrived

Responsibilities multiplied

Expectations grew

Time shrank

You learned to speak less.
React less.
Explain less.

Because explaining costs energy — and energy is scarce.

You didn't become distant.

You became tired.

Friends Say It Differently

Scene — Old Friend Meet-Up

Friend (laughing):
"Bro, you were wild before marriage. Now look at you."

Everyone laughs.

You smile.

But inside, something tightens.

Because they don't see the nights you chose responsibility over fun.
They don't see the dreams you postponed — not killed — postponed.

They call it change.

You call it growth with pain.

The Wife Notices It Too — But Differently

One night, quietly…

Wife:
"You don't talk like before."

Him:
"I'm just thinking."

Wife:
"You're always thinking."

You want to say:

I'm thinking about money.

About the future.
About not failing you.
About not disappointing anyone.

But you say nothing.

Because sometimes silence feels safer than misunderstanding.

The Inner Trial — Are They Right?

Late at night, when everyone sleeps, the accusation comes back.

Have I changed?
Am I colder?
Am I less loving?
Did I lose myself?

You replay old memories.

You were lighter.
You were more carefree.

But you were also less responsible.

You didn't lose yourself.

You expanded yourself — and expansion hurts.

Men Don't Change — They Compress

Men don't become heartless.

They compress emotions to function.

They reduce joy to keep stability.
They reduce complaints to keep peace.
They reduce dreams to meet reality.

This compression looks like change from outside.

But inside, it feels like pressure.

The Cruel Irony

The irony is brutal:

You change to protect

You change to provide

You change to survive

And then you're told:

"You have changed."

As if change is betrayal.

As if staying the same was ever possible.

The Anger You Never Express

There is anger.

Not explosive.
Not violent.

Quiet anger.

Anger that says:

Do you know how hard I'm trying?
Do you know what I'm carrying alone?
Do you know how many times I chose duty over desire?

But you swallow it.

Because anger doesn't fix misunderstandings.

The Loneliest Realization

One day, you realize something painful:

The man you are becoming will never fully be understood by the people who loved the man you were.

And that realization hurts more than criticism.

Because you didn't abandon them.

You just evolved.

Change Is the Price of Responsibility

Marriage doesn't steal freedom.

It redefines it.

Freedom now looks like:

Stability

Commitment

Long-term thinking

Emotional restraint

That's not loss.

That's maturity.

Even if it feels heavy.

What Every Man Wishes Someone Would Say

Not:

"You have changed."

But:

"I see how much you're carrying."
"I see how hard you're trying."
"I see the man you're becoming."

Those words don't inflate ego.

They heal wounds.

If You Are Reading This — Pause

If this chapter feels uncomfortable…

Good.

That means it's touching something real.

You didn't change because you failed.

You changed because life demanded more of you — and you stepped up.

The Truth No One Says Aloud

Every man on earth changes after marriage.

Not because marriage breaks him.

But because responsibility reshapes him.

And reshaping is painful.

But it is also powerful.

Closing Reflection

If someone tells you:

"You have changed after marriage."

Take a breath.

And remind yourself:

You didn’t change for less.
You changed for more.

More responsibility.
More love.
More weight.
More life.

And that change — even if misunderstood —
is the quiet proof of your strength.

5 'Your Family Should Understand You Are Married Now'

This sentence sounds simple.

Almost reasonable.
Almost practical.

"Your family should understand you are married now."

But behind it lives a pain most people don't slow down enough to see.

Because marriage doesn't just change a man's life.

It uproots a woman's entire world.

The Day She Left Everything She Knew

A man changes houses.

A woman changes homes.

She leaves:

the room where she grew up

the window she leaned on during teenage dreams

the kitchen where her mother knew her hunger without asking

the place where her name was spoken without explanation

And she walks into a house where everything is unfamiliar.

Not hostile.
Just unfamiliar.

And unfamiliar is frightening.

What People Call "Adjustment" Is Actually Grief

They say:

"She needs time to adjust."

But no one calls it what it really is.

Grief.

Grief for:

her routines

her independence

her comfort

her identity

She doesn't cry loudly.

She smiles.

And that smile is often misunderstood as strength — when it's actually survival.

The Man She Married Is Still Almost a Stranger

Love stories make it sound romantic.

Reality is quieter.

She married a man she chose — or accepted — but still hardly knows in daily life.

She doesn't yet know:

how he reacts when tired

how he behaves when angry

how he handles pressure

how much space he needs to feel safe

And yet, she has to trust him with her entire future.

That takes courage no one applauds.

The First Night in a New House

Scene — Bedroom, First Week After Marriage

She lies awake.

The room smells different.
The walls feel unfamiliar.

Her phone lights up.

Mother (text):
“Did you eat properly?”

She types:

“Yes, Ma.”

She deletes the next message she wanted to send:

I miss you.
I’m scared.
I don’t know how to belong here yet.

She turns off the phone.

That is sacrifice.

When Your Family Doesn't Mean to Hurt — But Does

Your family loves you.

They are not villains.

But they don't realize that every casual comment carries weight.

"In our house, we do things this way."
"This is how it has always been."
"She will learn slowly."

They say it casually.

She hears it deeply.

Because she is trying — every single day — to learn without making mistakes.

The Silence She Chooses Over Complaints

She notices everything.

The tone

The comparisons

The unspoken expectations

But she rarely speaks.

Not because she has nothing to say.

But because she doesn't want to create distance between you and your family.

So she absorbs discomfort quietly.

That silence is not weakness.

It is love.

The Inner Conflict No One Asks About

Inside her, a battle runs constantly:

If I speak, I'll be called sensitive.
If I stay silent, I'll slowly disappear.
If I complain, I'll hurt him.
If I don't, I'll hurt myself.

So she compromises — again.

Not because she is powerless.

But because she values peace more than victory.

"Your Family Should Understand" Is Not Rejection

When she says:

"Your family should understand you are married now."

She is not asking you to abandon them.

She is asking for space to exist without fear.

She is asking for:

boundaries, not walls

respect, not rebellion

partnership, not separation

She wants to feel safe — emotionally — in the life she chose.

The Man's Conflict Is Real — But So Is Hers

Yes, you are torn between love and loyalty.

But she is torn between:

gratitude and pain

adjustment and identity

respect and self-respect

She doesn't want to replace your family.

She just wants to belong somewhere without constantly proving herself.

The Weight of Being "The New One"

She is always:

careful

alert

observing

One wrong word can be misinterpreted.
One mistake can be remembered.

She learns slowly — not because she is incapable — but because fear slows learning.

And fear lives quietly in new spaces.

Love Looks Different for a Woman After Marriage

She loves by:

adapting

compromising

observing

adjusting her tone

controlling her emotions

Her sacrifices don't look dramatic.

They look ordinary.

Which makes them easy to ignore.

What Every Woman Hopes Her Husband Will Do

Not fight.
Not argue.
Not choose sides.

Just this:

Stand beside her when it matters.

Not loudly.
Not angrily.

But firmly.

So she knows she is not alone in unfamiliar territory.

When a Man Understands This — Everything Changes

When you truly understand what she left behind…

- you listen more patiently

you protect more gently

you speak more thoughtfully

you create boundaries naturally

You don't feel forced.

You feel responsible.

Marriage Is Not About Who Sacrifices More

It's not a competition.

Men sacrifice.
Women sacrifice.

But sacrifices look different.

Understanding begins when comparison ends.

This Is Not Just Her Story — It's Ours

Every woman who left her home carries this story.

Every man who loves deeply must understand it.

Because marriage isn't just about joining families.

It's about creating safety for two people who chose each other.

Closing Reflection

When someone says:

"Your family should understand you are married now."

Listen closely.

It is not anger.

It is vulnerability asking for protection.

And when a man becomes that protection — not with force, but with empathy — marriage stops feeling like adjustment…

And starts feeling like home.

When Love Turns Quiet – The Slow Drift Nobody Notices

Love rarely breaks in one loud moment.

It fades quietly.
Between unfinished conversations.
Between "later" and "tomorrow."
Between exhaustion and misunderstanding.

No one announces it.
No one plans it.

It just… happens.

The Silence That Didn't Exist Before

There was a time when silence felt comfortable.
Now it feels heavy.
You sit in the same room.
Phones in hand.
TV murmuring in the background.

But your minds are elsewhere.

Not angry.
Not fighting.

Just… distant.

And distance is far more dangerous than conflict.

When Talking Feels Like Work

You still talk.

About groceries.
Bills.
Plans.

But not about feelings.

Because feelings take energy.
And both of you are already tired.

So you choose peace over honesty.
Silence over explanation.

And slowly, the emotional connection starts starving.

The Man's Inner Conflict

Inside him, thoughts pile up:

If I speak, it may become an argument.
If I stay silent, at least the house is calm.

So he stays quiet.

He convinces himself:

This is maturity.
This is sacrifice.

But silence doesn't dissolve emotions.

It stores them.

The Woman's Quiet Loneliness

She notices first.

She always does.

She notices:

fewer questions

shorter replies

less eye contact

affection that feels scheduled

She asks once.

Wife:
"Is everything okay between us?"

Him:
"Yes. Just tired."

She nods.

But something inside her folds in on itself.
Because tiredness has become the answer to everything.

Love Doesn't Die — It Suffocates

Love needs air.

Conversation.
Laughter.
Small arguments.
Small repairs.

When those stop, love doesn't explode.

It suffocates quietly.

Like a plant watered less and less — not enough to die quickly, but enough to weaken daily.

When Responsibility Replaces Romance

Responsibilities multiply.

Romance doesn't.

You think:

We'll fix this when things settle down.

But life doesn't settle.

It only moves faster.

And romance doesn't survive on intention alone.

It needs attention.

The First Time You Feel Like Roommates

It hits suddenly.

Not dramatically.

Just a realization:

We function well… but do we feel close?

You share a house.
A bed.

A life.

But not always your inner worlds.

And that realization scares you — but you don’t say it.

Because you don’t know how.

Love Needs Courage Too

People think courage is needed to start relationships.

But courage is needed even more to maintain them.

Courage to say:

"I feel disconnected."

"I miss us."

"I don't want to lose this."

Silence feels safe.
Honesty feels risky.

But silence slowly kills what honesty could save.

The Missed Moments

Small moments pass unnoticed:
A story she wanted to tell

A thought he wanted to share

A laugh that died halfway

Not because of lack of love.

Because of lack of presence.

The Day You Almost Say It

One evening, you almost say:

"I feel far from you."

But then:

the phone rings

the child cries

the moment passes

And you promise yourself:

Next time.

But next time keeps getting postponed.

Understanding Is a Daily Choice

Love is not sustained by grand gestures.

It's sustained by:

daily listening

daily patience

daily effort

Not perfection.

Just showing up emotionally — even when tired.

Reconnection Starts Small

Reconnection doesn't need speeches.

It needs:

one honest question

one uninterrupted conversation

one shared silence without phones

Small steps.

Taken consistently.

It's Not Too Late — Unless You Decide It Is

Most relationships don't end because love disappeared.

They end because communication stopped trying.

As long as both hearts are still willing…

There is hope.

Closing Reflection

If love feels quiet right now…

Don't panic.

Quiet doesn't mean gone.

It means waiting to be heard again.

Speak.

Listen.

Stay.

Because love that survives silence becomes stronger — but only if someone is brave enough to break it.

6 Financial Awakening – Carrying a Mountain for the First Time

There is a moment in every man's life when money stops being a number and becomes a weight.

Not a dramatic moment.
No announcement.
No warning.

Just a quiet realization that settles into your chest and refuses to leave.

You are no longer earning for comfort.
You are earning for survival, stability, dignity, and tomorrow.

And tomorrow suddenly feels very expensive.

Before marriage, money came and went. You worried, yes—but lightly. If something went wrong, someone else stood behind you. A family. A cushion. A silent safety net you never thanked because you never saw it.

After marriage, that net disappears.

Not because anyone took it away.

But because you stepped forward.

And now, if you fall, there is no one beneath you.
Only people depending on you not to.

That is when money becomes heavy.

The first bill hits differently.

You stare at it longer than necessary. Not because you don't understand it—but because you understand it too well. Rent. EMI. Groceries. Electricity. Internet. Medical. Unexpected expenses that arrive without permission.

You calculate again and again, hoping the numbers will magically change.

They don't.

You don't say anything. You just exhale quietly.

Your wife may be sitting nearby, scrolling on her phone or folding clothes. She senses something but doesn't ask. You smile and say, "It's fine."

That word—fine—starts doing a lot of emotional work in your life.

You remember a time when salary day felt exciting.

Now it feels like relief.

Money comes in—and before you even touch it, it already belongs somewhere else. Bills claim it. Responsibilities divide it. Future plans quietly reserve it.

There is no "extra" anymore.

And if there is, you feel guilty spending it on yourself.

You look at something you want to buy—shoes, a phone, a small indulgence—and your mind immediately asks, Is this necessary?

You close the app.

You didn't become less ambitious.
You became more aware.

Nights change too.

You lie in bed beside your wife, lights off, house quiet. She sleeps quickly—her breathing soft and steady.

You stare at the ceiling.

Your mind runs numbers instead of dreams.

What if something happens?
What if I lose my job?
What if I can't provide enough?
What if I fail?

No one taught you how to sleep with responsibility pressing on your chest like a stone.

You turn to the side so she won't notice you're awake again.

You start noticing your father differently.

How he used to sit silently after dinner.
How he worried without speaking.
How he chose function over comfort.

You finally understand him.

Not because someone explained it to you—but because you became him.

And that understanding is both humbling and terrifying.

Your wife sacrifices too, even if money is not in her hands.

She calculates expenses before speaking.
She avoids asking for things she wants.
She says, “We can manage,” when she knows it will be tight.

Sometimes she says nothing—and that hurts you more than if she complained.

Because now you know she is adjusting around your limitations.

And that hurts your pride, even though it shouldn’t.

There are moments when frustration leaks out.

A small argument over spending.
A tone that sharpens unexpectedly.
Silence that lasts longer than it should.

Later, alone, you realize it was never about money.

It was about pressure.

Pressure to be strong.
Pressure to be sufficient.
Pressure to never say, “I’m scared.”

Men aren’t taught to talk about financial fear.
They’re taught to solve it quietly.

Sometimes your mother calls and asks casually, "Everything okay?"

You say yes.

She hears the pause before your answer but chooses not to press.

She knows that pause.

She lived it for years.

The hardest part of financial awakening is not lack.

It's responsibility without reassurance.

No one sits you down and says, You're doing enough.

No one tells you, This fear is normal.

So you keep going, unsure, carrying the mountain step by step.

But somewhere along the way, something changes inside you.

You become sharper.
More aware.
More grounded.

You stop chasing comfort and start building security.

It's not glamorous.
It doesn't look successful from outside.

But it is real growth.

Painful growth.

One day, much later, you'll look back at this phase and realize:

This was the moment you became a provider—not just of money, but of stability.

You carried fear silently so others could feel safe.

You learned restraint so others could have certainty.

You grew heavier so others could sleep lighter.

If you're reading this and feeling seen—pause.

Take a breath.

You are not weak for feeling this pressure.

You are becoming something stronger than you were before.

And no one may clap for this phase of your life.

But this is where real men are built—quietly, honestly, under the weight of responsibility they never asked for but chose to carry anyway.

This is not just your story.

This is the story of every man who woke up one day and realized—

I am the safety net now.

The Loneliness No One Talks About

There is a loneliness that doesn't come from being alone.

It comes from being needed by everyone…
and understood by no one.

After marriage, your world fills with people.
Responsibilities.
Voices.
Expectations.

Yet somehow, you begin to disappear inside all of it.

Not suddenly.
Not dramatically.

Slowly. Quietly. Invisibly.

You still laugh.
You still talk.
You still show up.

But fewer people ask how you are really doing.

And even when they do, you don't know how to answer honestly anymore.

So you say what you've practiced saying:

"I'm fine."

Loneliness for a man doesn't look like isolation.

It looks like strength.

It looks like handling things alone.

Solving problems quietly.
Absorbing stress without complaint.

From the outside, you look stable.

Inside, you feel like a room no one enters anymore.

Your wife loves you.
Your family needs you.
Your workplace depends on you.

But who do you lean on?

You can’t burden your wife—she already adjusts so much.
You can’t worry your parents—they sacrificed too much already.
You can’t open up to friends—everyone is busy fighting their own battles.

So you become your own support system.

And that’s exhausting.

At night, when the house finally sleeps, that’s when the loneliness speaks.

Not loudly.

Softly.

It asks questions you avoid during the day.

When did I stop feeling light?
When did I stop sharing my fears?
When did I become the strong one who never needs help?

You don’t answer.

You just turn to the other side and close your eyes.

Sometimes your wife notices the distance.

She asks, gently, "Are you okay?"

You want to say so much.

But words feel risky.

What if she worries?
What if she misunderstands?
What if she thinks you're unhappy with her?

So you choose the safer option.

"I'm just tired."

And the loneliness grows—not because she doesn't care, but because you don't know how to let her in without everything falling apart.

You start missing your old self.

Not because that life was better.

But because that version of you was simpler.

He laughed more easily.
He worried less deeply.
He didn't carry invisible pressure in his chest.

You don't want to go back.

You just want to feel seen again.

There are days you feel numb.

Not sad.
Not angry.

Just empty.

You go through routines efficiently—like a machine that works perfectly but feels nothing.

And that scares you more than pain ever did.

Because pain reminds you that you're alive.

Numbness makes you wonder if you're slowly fading.

Men are rarely taught how to ask for emotional help.

They are taught to be reliable.
To be steady.
To be the one others lean on.

So when loneliness arrives, they don't ask for company.

They learn to live with it.

But here is the truth no one tells you:

Loneliness doesn't mean you are ungrateful.
It doesn't mean you don't love your family.
It doesn't mean something is wrong with you.

It means you are human.

It means you've been strong for too long without rest.

If you're reading this and feeling a tightness in your chest, pause.

You are not weak for feeling lonely in a full house.
You are not broken for needing emotional space.
You are not failing because you feel tired of being strong.

You are carrying more than you were ever taught how to carry.

Loneliness doesn't disappear overnight.

But it softens when you allow yourself one honest moment.

One real conversation.
One shared fear.
One admission that says, "I don't have it all together."

Strength isn't silence forever.
Strength is knowing when to speak.
And if no one has told you this yet, let this book say it clearly:

You matter beyond what you provide.
You deserve understanding, not just responsibility.
You are allowed to feel lonely—even while being loved.

This chapter isn't here to fix you.

It's here to remind you that you are not alone in feeling alone.

7 Ego, Love, and the Debt Trap

There was a time when money was simple.

You earned it.
You spent some on yourself.
You saved a little.
You didn't overthink every rupee.

If you wanted something, you bought it.
If you were tired, you treated yourself.
If your pocket was empty, you laughed it off and waited for the next salary.

Back then, money was just money.

After marriage, money becomes meaning.

Now every rupee has a face.

Your wife's quiet wishes.
Your child's future dreams.
Your parents' expectations.
The roof over everyone's head.

Suddenly, spending a thousand rupees on yourself feels heavy.

You pause.
You calculate.
You close the app.
You tell yourself, "Later."

And that "later" keeps moving further away.

You still earn the same money, sometimes even more.

But now it never feels enough.

Because love has expanded your responsibilities in every direction.

You are no longer earning for your life.
You are earning for many lives at once.

You watch your wife carefully.

She never demands loudly.
She rarely asks dircctly.
But you notice the small things.

The dress she liked but didn't buy.
The phone she needs but says can wait.
The smile she forces when she says, "It's okay."

And something inside you breaks quietly.

You promise yourself: I will give her better than this.

Then come the children.

Tiny hands.
Big dreams.

School fees.
Books.
Uniforms.

Doctor visits.
Future plans you can't even fully imagine yet.

You look at your child sleeping and think,
I will never let you feel lack.

Even if it costs me everything.

Your parents are still there.

Aging.
Needing more care than before.
Medical expenses.
House repairs.
Social responsibilities.

They don't say much.
But you know they are counting on you.

You are the bridge holding generations together.

And bridges don't complain when people walk over them.

Slowly, silently, ego enters the picture.

Not the loud, arrogant ego.

The quiet male ego.

The one that says,
I should be able to manage this.
I shouldn't ask for help.
I can handle it.

So when money falls short, you don't talk.

You calculate again.

And then… you take a loan.

At first, it feels temporary.

Just a small amount.
Just for now.
Just until things improve.

You don't tell your wife.
You don't tell your parents.
You don't tell anyone.

Not because you don't trust them.

But because you don't want to worry them.

And somewhere deeper, because admitting it feels like failure.

You tell yourself, I'll manage.

You always do.

Then another need appears.

A better house.
A safer neighbourhood.
A good school.
A medical emergency.

Another loan.

Another EMI.

Another silent burden added to your chest.

You stop buying things for yourself completely.

New clothes feel unnecessary.

Old shoes feel "still usable."
Hobbies slowly disappear.

You don't even notice when you stop asking,
What do I want?

Because the answer no longer matters.

Your life becomes work, responsibility, calculation.

You stay busy on purpose.

Busy means you don't think.
Busy means you don't feel the weight.
Busy means you don't have to face the fear.

The fear that one day, this mountain might be too heavy.

At night, when everyone sleeps, you stare at the ceiling.

Numbers run in your head.
EMIs.
Due dates.
Salary days.

You don't feel anger.

You feel responsibility.

And responsibility doesn't scream.

It sits quietly on your chest and makes breathing harder.

Your wife senses something.

She asks, "Is everything okay financially?"

You smile.

"Yeah, don't worry."

You mean it.

Because worrying her feels worse than carrying the stress alone.

Sometimes people say,
"You've changed."

Yes.

You have.

You became someone who thinks a thousand times before spending a single rupee on himself,
but never thinks twice before spending it on his family.

You became someone who sacrifices comfort silently,
so others can live peacefully.

This is the debt trap no one talks about.

Not just financial debt.

Emotional debt.

The debt of expectations.
The debt of love.
The debt of being "the man who will manage."

And you pay it daily—with your peace.

But here is the truth this world rarely says out loud:

This sacrifice doesn't make you weak.
This silence doesn't make you small.
This struggle doesn't mean you failed.

It means you loved deeply.

It means you chose your family over yourself again and again.

Still, even the strongest man needs space to breathe.

Love should not always mean suffering alone.
Responsibility should not always mean silence.
Providing should not mean disappearing.

If you see yourself in these lines, pause for a moment.

You are not alone.
You are not foolish.
You are not invisible.

You are doing the hardest job—loving silently.

And this book sees you.

Not as a wallet.
Not as a machine.
But as a human being who carries ego, love, fear, and hope all at once.

This chapter isn't asking you to stop caring.

It's reminding you that you matter too.

Even the man who holds everyone together deserves understanding.

And sometimes…
sharing the weight is not weakness.

It's survival.

When Strength Becomes a Habit, Not a Choice

At first, strength feels heroic.

You stand taller.
You take charge.
You feel proud that people depend on you.

But slowly, without you noticing, strength stops being a choice.

It becomes a habit.

And habits don't ask whether you are tired.

You wake up every morning with a checklist already running in your head.

Bills.
Work pressure.
Family needs.
Future planning.

Even before your feet touch the floor, your mind is already working overtime.

There is no pause button anymore.

You don't ask, "Do I have the energy for this?"
You ask, "How do I manage this?"

Because managing is what you do now.

People admire you.

They say things like,
"He is very responsible."
"He handles everything so well."
"He never panics."

They don't see what it costs you.

Because you've trained yourself to hide the cracks.

You smile at family gatherings.
You laugh at jokes.
You give advice to others.

But inside, there's a quiet exhaustion that never fully leaves.

Not physical tiredness.

A deeper one.

The kind sleep doesn't fix.

You remember a time when you could say no.

When you could rest without guilt.
When you could fail without feeling like the whole system would collapse.

Now, even the idea of slowing down feels dangerous.

If you stop, who will handle things?

Your inner voice doesn't shout.

It whispers.

Just push a little more.
You've handled worse.
You can't afford to break.

And so you don't.

There are moments when emotions try to surface.

A lump in the throat.
A heaviness behind the eyes.

You swallow it.

Not because you're heartless.

But because crying feels like opening a door you're not sure you can close again.

Your wife notices your silence.

She asks why you don't talk like before.

You don't have an answer.

How do you explain that you're not silent because you don't care…

…but because you are carrying too much?

Every good moment is followed by a calculation.

Can I afford this joy?
What comes next?

Strength has trained you to stay alert all the time.

Relaxation feels unfamiliar.
Peace feels temporary.

You're always waiting for the next problem.

This is the unseen cost of being "the strong one."

You don't fall apart dramatically.
You slowly disappear behind responsibility.

And yet, despite everything, you keep going.

Because love doesn't let you stop.
Because duty doesn't let you rest.
Because hope—quiet, stubborn hope—keeps whispering that one day

things will feel lighter.

If you're reading this and feeling tired in a way you can't explain, let this chapter sit with you.

You are not lazy.
You are not ungrateful.
You are not weak.

You are strong in a way that rarely gets acknowledged.

But remember this—strength doesn't mean silence forever.

Even the strongest pillar needs support, or it cracks silently.

And you…
you deserve support too.

The Day He Stops Talking About Himself

There is a quiet moment in a man's life when he realizes something painful.

He no longer talks about himself.

Not his dreams.
Not his fears.
Not his unfinished wishes.

Because somewhere along the way, his life became a background service—always running, never visible.

Earlier, when people asked, "How are you?"
He used to answer honestly.

Now he replies automatically.

"Fine."
"Busy."
"All good."

Not lies.
Just incomplete truths.

You notice it first in conversations.

Friends talk about trips, plans, ambitions.
You listen.
You nod.
You smile.

But you don't add much.

Because your dreams don't sound exciting anymore.

They sound heavy.

School fees.
Loan closure.
Medical security.
A stable future.

Practical dreams don't impress people.

So you keep them to yourself.

At home, your wife talks about the house, the child, the future.

You listen carefully.

You encourage her.
You reassure her.

But when it's your turn to speak…
you say nothing important.

Because your worries feel like burdens you don't want to place on her shoulders.

Slowly, you stop asking yourself questions like:

What do I want?
What makes me happy?
What am I missing?

Because answering them would open doors you don't have time to walk through.

Your identity shifts quietly.

You are no longer you.

You are:

Someone's husband.
Someone's father.
Someone's son.
Someone's provider.

All noble roles.

All demanding.

And somehow, none of them ask who you are becoming inside.

You don't feel angry about it.

That's the strange part.

You feel… resigned.

Like a soldier who accepted the mission and stopped counting the days.

Sometimes you look at old photos.

A younger version of you smiles freely.

You don't miss his freedom.

You miss his lightness.

There are moments—small, unexpected—when your old self tries to surface.

A song you once loved.
A hobby you abandoned.
A random thought that excites you.

And for a second, you feel alive again.

Then responsibility taps your shoulder.

And you go back.

People assume silence means peace.

But silence can also mean exhaustion.

It can mean you've spoken to yourself so much that you don't know what's worth saying out loud anymore.

You are not cold.

You are overloaded.

If you're reading this and thinking, This is exactly me, let me tell you something important:

You didn't lose yourself.

You paused yourself.

For love.
For family.
For duty.

And paused things can be resumed.

One honest conversation can bring pieces back.
One shared fear can lighten the load.
One moment of choosing yourself—without guilt—can remind you that you still exist beyond responsibility.

You don't need to reclaim your whole life at once.

Just your voice.

Just your truth.

Just one sentence that starts with,
"Let me tell you how I really feel."

Because the man who stopped talking about himself didn't disappear.

He just learned to be quiet.

And quiet men carry the loudest stories inside them.

8 Compatibility Is Not Romance, It Is Understanding

Romance is loud.

It posts photos.
It remembers dates.
It speaks sweet words in public.

Compatibility is quiet.

It notices silence.
It understands tired eyes.
It hears the words that were never spoken.

And most people confuse the two.

In the beginning, love feels effortless.

You talk for hours.
You laugh easily.
You promise without fear.

Back then, understanding feels automatic—because life hasn't tested you yet.

After marriage, reality enters the room.

And romance alone cannot survive reality.

Only understanding can.

Understanding means knowing that love looks different on tired days.

That care sometimes comes as silence, not sweet words.
That sacrifice doesn't always announce itself.

But how do you explain that to someone who is hurting?

You come home late.

Not because you don't want to be with her.
But because you're trying to hold everything together.

Work pressure.
Financial stress.
Family responsibility.

Your mind is exhausted before your body reaches home.

You don't notice the tone of your voice.
You don't realize your face looks distant.

And that distance hurts her.

She doesn't see your battles.

She only feels your absence.

So she calls someone.

A friend.
A sister.
Someone who will listen.

You're standing outside the room.

The door is half closed.

You weren't trying to listen.

You were just passing by.

Then you hear your name.

He has changed after marriage."

Your feet stop moving.

He doesn't take care of me the way he should."

Your chest tightens.

He was so sweet before. Now he's always busy. Always tired."

Your throat goes dry.

"Sometimes I feel like he doesn't even love me anymore."

And then the sentence that breaks something inside you:

"I don't think he is suitable for me."

You don't breathe.

You don't move.

You don't interrupt.

You just stand there…
as the man you became for her is quietly erased by words.

She keeps talking.

"He pretended to be caring before marriage."

"Now I'm seeing his real face."
"He's rude."
"He doesn't understand me."

Each word lands on you like a verdict.

And the most painful part?

She doesn't know you're listening.

So these words are honest.

You think of everything you've given up.

Your personal dreams.
Your comforts.
Your freedom.
Your sleep.

You think of the thousand times you chose responsibility over rest.
Family over self.
Silence over argument.

And suddenly, none of it seems visible.

You don't feel angry.

You feel… small.

Like all your sacrifices were invisible.

Like your love failed to translate.

You step back quietly.

Because what do you say?

How do you explain pain without sounding defensive?

How do you explain silence without sounding careless?

So you choose the only option you've practiced well.

You stay quiet.

You go to the washroom.

Lock the door.

Turn on the tap.

And cry.

Not loudly.

Silently.

Because even your tears have learned to be careful.

You cry for the man you used to be.
You cry for the man you are trying to become.
You cry because being misunderstood hurts more than being tired.

This is where compatibility matters more than romance.

Because romance would say,
"He should be more expressive."

Compatibility asks,
"Why is he so quiet lately?"

Romance complains.
Compatibility observes.

Understanding doesn't mean agreeing with everything.

It means pausing before judging.

It means asking,
"Are you okay?"
instead of saying,
"You've changed."

A man can survive pressure.

What breaks him is feeling unappreciated while sacrificing everything.

Feeling accused while loving deeply.

Feeling alone inside a marriage.

If you're reading this and your eyes are wet, let me tell you something gently:

You are not heartless.
You are not pretending.
You are not a bad man.

You are a tired man who loved quietly.

Compatibility is not about constant happiness.

It is about patience on bad days.

It is about noticing effort that doesn't come with flowers or words.

It is about understanding that love sometimes looks like exhaustion.

If she had opened the door and seen you standing there…

If she had seen your eyes…

Maybe the conversation would have been different.

But life doesn't always give explanations.

Sometimes it gives silence.

And the strongest men are the ones who carry that silence without turning bitter.

If this chapter feels like it was written from your own life, pause.

You are not alone in this pain.

There are millions of men standing quietly outside half-closed doors,
loving deeply,
hurting silently,
and still choosing to stay.

Compatibility begins the day both hearts decide to understand before accusing.

And love survives only where understanding lives.

This book sees you.

The man who cried quietly…
and still showed up the next morning.

The Day He Realizes Love Needs Translation

Love does not disappear.

It just starts speaking a language no one taught you.

You loved her the only way you knew how.

By working harder.
By worrying more.
By planning for the future instead of enjoying the present.

You thought love meant protection.

She thought love meant presence.

Neither of you were wrong.

You were just speaking different languages.

After that night—after those words accidentally heard through a half-closed door—something inside you changed.

Not bitterness.

Awareness.

You started noticing things you had ignored before.

The way she waits for you to finish work and talk.
The way her voice drops when you don’t respond much.
The way she smiles but her eyes ask questions.

You realize something painful and important at the same time.

She wasn’t complaining because she hates you.

She was complaining because she misses you.

Understanding doesn't arrive like a movie scene.

There's no dramatic apology.
No emotional speech.

Just quiet realizations.

And guilt.

Not the loud kind.

The heavy kind.

You replay moments in your head.

Times you answered with "hmm" instead of listening.
Times you were physically present but mentally somewhere else.
Times you assumed she understood your stress without you explaining it.

You assumed.

She waited.

Men are taught to show love by doing.

Women often feel love through sharing.

And no one teaches couples how to bridge that gap.

You sit alone one night.

Not crying this time.

Thinking.

You ask yourself a hard question:

When was the last time I told her what I'm carrying?

Not complaints.
Not instructions.

Truth.

You realize you tried to be strong for her…

when what she needed was honesty with her.

The next day, you come home tired again.

Nothing has changed outside.

Same responsibilities.
Same pressures.

But something inside you shifts.

She asks, “How was your day?”

You almost say, “Fine.”

Almost.

Then you stop.

You take a breath.

“It was heavy,” you say quietly.

She looks at you differently.

Not offended.

Surprised.

You don’t explain everything.

You don’t need to.

That one sentence does something powerful.

It opens a door.

You talk slowly.

Awkwardly.

Not like a romantic hero.

Like a human.

You tell her you feel pressure.
That you feel scared sometimes.
That you don't always know how to express love without feeling weak.

She listens.

Really listens.

Her eyes fill.

Not with anger.

With understanding.

She says, "I didn't know you felt so much."

And that sentence heals something in you.

Love didn't need more sacrifice.

It needed translation.

You learn something important that night.

Compatibility isn't about perfection.

It's about effort in understanding each other's emotional language.

You still work hard.
You still carry responsibility.

But now, you carry less alone.

If you're reading this and thinking, I wish someone understood me like that, let this be your reminder:

Your love is real.
Your effort matters.
But love grows strongest when it is explained, not assumed.

Men don't lose love because they stop caring.

They lose love because they stop expressing what caring looks like inside them.

You don't need grand gestures.

You need shared truth.

And shared truth begins with one honest sentence.

This chapter isn't telling you to change who you are.

It's telling you to let your partner see who you are beneath the strength.

Because love that understands both silence and speech…

That love lasts.

When He Finally Breaks—and Doesn't Apologize for It

Every man reaches a point where holding on becomes heavier than letting go.

Not letting go of love.
Not letting go of responsibility.

Letting go of the act.

For years, you carried everything quietly.

You learned how to smile while drowning.
How to reassure others while feeling uncertain.
How to be strong even when your hands were shaking inside.

You never complained.

Not because you didn't feel pain.

But because you believed pain was part of the job.

Men aren't taught how to fall apart safely.

They're taught how to endure.

So when breaking finally happens, it doesn't look dramatic.

It looks like silence.

It happens on an ordinary day.

No big fight.
No big loss.

Just one extra sentence.
One extra demand.

One extra expectation.

And something inside you finally says, Enough.

Your wife notices you're quieter than usual.

She asks what's wrong.

You try to answer lightly.

But your voice cracks.

And suddenly, everything you buried starts rising.

Not as anger.

As truth.

"I'm tired," you say.

Not tired from work.

Tired from carrying expectations.
Tired from being strong.
Tired from proving love through sacrifice instead of words.

You don't shout.

You don't accuse.

You don't blame.

You just speak.

And that honesty feels terrifying.

You admit things you've never said out loud.

That you feel pressure all the time.

That you're scared of failing your family.
That sometimes you feel invisible even while being needed.

That you didn't stop loving—
you just stopped knowing how to show it.

You expect disappointment.

Anger.

Judgment.

Instead… she listens.

Not interrupting.

Not defending.

Listening.

She realizes something she never fully saw before.

That your silence wasn't distance.

It was weight.

She cries too.

Not because she's hurt.

But because she finally understands.

That moment doesn't fix everything.

But it changes the direction.

For the first time, you don't apologize for being tired.

You don't apologize for feeling overwhelmed.

You don't apologize for being human.

And that's when healing quietly begins.

You learn that strength doesn't disappear when you speak.

It deepens.

Because now it's shared.

You still have responsibilities.

Still have pressure.

Still have days when things feel too much.

But now, you're not alone inside it.

If you're reading this and thinking, I wish I could say all this, let me tell you something clearly:

Breaking doesn't make you weak.

Breaking honestly makes you real.

You don't have to collapse to be heard.

You just have to stop hiding.

This chapter is for every man who carried everything without complaint
until his silence became too loud to ignore.

You didn't fail.

You finally spoke.

And sometimes, that's the bravest thing a man can do.

9 Joint Family – A Dream That Needs Effort From All

A joint family is a beautiful dream.

Grandparents in the corner of the house,
children running freely,
shared meals, shared laughter, shared memories.

On paper, it looks perfect.

In real life, it survives only on one thing—effort.

And effort is something everyone must give, not just one person.

A joint family is not built by love alone.

It is built by patience.
By tolerance.
By the ability to ignore small things before they become big wounds.

But this is where things slowly start breaking.

After marriage, a man stands in the middle of two worlds.

The home he was born into.

And the home he is building.

Both expect him to balance perfectly.

Both expect him to understand.
Both expect him to adjust.

And when balance fails, he becomes the rope in a tug of war.

Small issues start quietly.

Food preferences.
Habits.
Tone of voice.
Different ways of doing the same thing.

Nothing big.

Nothing unfixable.

But instead of correcting with love, people complain.
Instead of understanding, they accuse.
Instead of patience, they choose ego.

A mother feels disrespected.

A wife feels suffocated.

A sister feels ignored.
A brother feels misunderstood.

And the man?
He feels helpless.

He tries to explain gently.

"Please adjust a little."
"Please ignore this small thing."

"She didn't mean it."
"He didn't say it intentionally."

But explanations don't always heal.

Sometimes they add fuel.

Slowly, the house fills with silence.

Not peaceful silence.

Tense silence.

The kind where everyone speaks softly but thinks loudly.

People stop correcting mistakes lovingly.

They start collecting them.

Every past issue becomes a weapon.

Every small habit becomes proof of disrespect.

And one day, someone says the sentence that changes everything:

"Let's live separately."

It sounds practical.
It sounds peaceful.

But it feels like a funeral.

A man never imagines leaving the house where he grew up.

The walls that heard his childhood laughter.
The mother who waited for him every night.
The family that shaped him.

But sometimes, he leaves not because he wants to…

but because peace demands a sacrifice.

And when he leaves, no one really wins.

The wife loses the warmth of a bigger family.
The parents lose daily closeness to their son.
The siblings lose shared moments.

And the man loses something deeper.

A part of his identity.

What hurts most is knowing it could have been avoided.

If someone had ignored one sentence.
If someone had corrected gently instead of shouting.
If someone had said, "It's okay, next time take care."

A joint family doesn't break because of big problems.

It breaks because of small things handled badly.

No one teaches us how to live together after marriage.

No one teaches a wife how difficult it is to adjust to a new house.
No one teaches parents how much pressure their son is under.
No one teaches siblings how to step back sometimes.

Everyone expects love.

Few are ready to practice it.

Love in a joint family is not about perfection.

It is about tolerance.

About choosing peace over proving a point.

About correcting mistakes with kindness, not humiliation.

A peaceful house is not one without mistakes.

It is one where mistakes are handled with maturity.

If you're reading this and remembering arguments, tears, separations—pause.

Maybe you were hurt.
Maybe you were right.

But was the relationship worth losing?

A joint family is not a prison.

And it is not heaven either.

It is a living system.

It survives only when everyone adjusts a little, ignores a little, forgives a little.

For the man in the middle, this chapter is a quiet apology.

For asking you to be strong all the time.

For expecting you to choose between people you love.

For the wife, this chapter is a reminder.

Adjustment doesn't mean losing yourself.
It means building peace slowly.

For the parents, this chapter is a request.

Your son is not choosing anyone over you.
He is just trying to hold everyone together.

For siblings, this chapter is a truth.

Support heals faster than blame.

If this chapter made your eyes wet, that's okay.

Some tears come from recognition, not weakness.

A joint family is still a beautiful dream.

But dreams need effort.

From all sides.

Only then does a house remain a home…
and not a battlefield disguised as tradition.

This book is not blaming anyone.

It is asking everyone to pause.

And choose understanding…
before separation becomes the only solution left.

The Silent Prayer of a Man

There is a prayer a man makes that he never speaks out loud.

Not in a temple.
Not in a mosque.
Not in a church.

He makes it while driving alone.
While lying awake at night.
While watching his family sleep.

He doesn't pray for himself.

He prays that everyone he loves stays okay.

That his parents remain healthy.
That his wife feels safe and loved.
That his children never feel the fear he hides behind his smile.

He prays that arguments don't turn into permanent wounds.
That misunderstandings don't become lifelong bitterness.
That his home doesn't break in ways that can never be repaired.

He prays quietly because he has learned something painful.

Not every prayer is answered with miracles.

Some are answered with endurance.

He has seen too much.

Families that stopped talking.
Brothers who became strangers.
Parents who grew old waiting for a call.

He doesn't want that future.

So he bends.
He adjusts.
He sacrifices.

Again and again.

Sometimes he feels like a negotiator, not a husband or son.

Explaining one side to the other.
Softening harsh words.
Hiding his own hurt so peace can survive.

He tells his wife, “They didn’t mean it.”
He tells his parents, “She’s still adjusting.”

And in between, he tells himself nothing.

There are nights when he feels empty.

Not angry.

Just tired of carrying everyone’s emotions like fragile glass.

One wrong move, and everything shatters.

Yet every morning, he wakes up and tries again.

Because love, for him, is not a feeling anymore.

It is responsibility.

He knows he can’t make everyone happy.

But he still tries.

Because giving up feels worse than failing.

If you're reading this and nodding quietly, let this chapter sit with you.

You are not invisible.
Your efforts are not meaningless.
Your silence is not weakness.

But hear this gently:

You are allowed to pray for yourself too.

You are allowed to want peace for your own heart.
You are allowed to rest without guilt.
You are allowed to say, "This is too much."

A family does not stay together because one man holds it tightly.

It stays together because everyone chooses understanding.

The silent prayer of a man should never be taken for granted.

Because behind that prayer is a heart that loves deeply,
even when it is exhausted.

If this chapter touched something inside you, don't rush past it.

Sit with it.

Some truths need quiet to be felt.

When He Smiles, But Something Inside Him Is Missing

There comes a stage in a man's life when his smile becomes automatic.

He smiles at work.
He smiles at family functions.
He smiles in photos.

And everyone assumes he is doing well.

But inside that smile, something is missing.

He is not unhappy.

That's the confusing part.

His family is there.
His responsibilities are being met.
Life is moving forward.

Yet something feels hollow.

Like a song playing without music.

He realizes this one day while laughing.

The laughter sounds right.
But it doesn't reach his chest.

And that's when he understands—
he has been living on duty for so long that joy has become optional.

He doesn't complain.

Because complaining feels disrespectful to everything he has.

He knows many have it worse.

So he keeps going.

But suppression has a cost.

It turns emotions flat.
It dulls excitement.
It makes days blend into each other.

Life becomes functional, not felt.

He notices he no longer reacts strongly to anything.

Good news comes—he nods.
Bad news comes—he manages.

He has trained himself too well.

Sometimes, his wife asks, “Why don’t you get excited anymore?”

He doesn’t know how to answer.

How do you explain emotional fatigue?

This is the stage where many men silently drift.

Not away from family.

Away from themselves.

They are present in body.
Absent in spirit.

Not because they don’t care.

But because caring consumed them.

This emptiness doesn’t scream.

It whispers.

And whispers are easy to ignore.

Until one day, something small brings tears.

A song.
A scene in a movie.
A memory.

And suddenly, emotions rush back like a flood.

He realizes he didn't lose them.

He buried them.

If you're reading this and feeling numb, pause.

Numbness is not strength.

It is a signal.

A signal that you've been strong for too long without release.

You don't need to change your life overnight.

You need to reconnect with yourself.

Slowly.

Gently.

Talk to someone you trust.
Do something that once made you feel alive.
Allow yourself moments without responsibility.

You are not betraying your family by choosing yourself occasionally.

You are preserving the man they love.

This chapter is a mirror.

If it reflects you, don't look away.

Your smile deserves to be real again.

Learning to Breathe Again

No one tells a man when he should stop holding his breath.

So he keeps holding it…
through responsibilities,
through expectations,
through years that pass quietly.

Until one day, he realizes he is exhausted—not because life is hard, but because he never allowed himself to exhale.

Learning to breathe again doesn't happen in one big moment.

It happens in small, almost invisible ways.

A slower walk home.
A deeper breath before answering.
A pause before saying yes to everything.

At first, it feels wrong.

Rest feels like laziness.
Silence feels like neglect.
Choosing yourself feels selfish.

Because you were taught that a good man gives, gives, gives—
and asks for nothing.

But something surprising happens when you begin to slow down.

The world doesn't collapse.

Your family doesn't fall apart.

In fact, things start feeling… lighter.

You begin speaking a little more.

Not complaining.

Sharing.

You say, "Today was heavy," and no one gets hurt.

You say, "I need some time," and the sky doesn't fall.

You realize something important.

You were afraid of disappointing people.

But in trying not to disappoint them, you disappointed yourself.

Learning to breathe again means accepting that you are human.

You have limits.
You have needs.
You have emotions that deserve space.

You start finding small joys again.

Tea that tastes warmer.
Music that feels deeper.
Laughter that comes naturally, not on command.

You don't abandon responsibility.

You balance it.

And balance feels different from sacrifice.

Your wife notices the change.

You are more present.

Not because you have fewer problems—

but because you're not carrying them alone anymore.

You learn that peace doesn't come from doing more.

It comes from being honest.

If you are reading this and breathing a little slower, that's good.

This chapter isn't about fixing your life.

It's about letting yourself live it.

Strength isn't holding your breath forever.

Strength is knowing when to breathe.

And if no one has told you this yet, let this book say it clearly:

You've done enough.
You are enough.
And it's okay to rest.

10 What Men Never Say

"I am tired."
"I am scared."
"I need support too."

These sentences don't disappear.

They die inside men.

Not because men don't feel them.

A man learns very early that his value is measured by how much he can carry.

How much pressure he can handle.
How many problems he can solve.
How many people can depend on him.

So when tiredness comes, he hides it.

Because tiredness sounds like weakness.

"I am tired" doesn't mean I don't want to try anymore.

It means I have been strong for too long without rest.

But men rarely say it.

Because once you say you are tired, someone might worry.

And men don't want to be the reason anyone worries.

"I am scared" is even harder.

Scared of failure.
Scared of not earning enough.
Scared of disappointing parents.
Scared of not being a good husband or father.

Men carry fear quietly.

They convert it into hard work.
Into silence.
Into sleepless nights.

Fear doesn't stop them.

It pushes them forward—
even when they are already exhausted.

"I need support too" almost never comes out.

Because men are taught that support flows from them, not to them.

They believe they must always be ready.

Ready to protect.
Ready to provide.
Ready to handle everything alone.

Saying "no" doesn't come naturally to them.

Not because they don't want boundaries.

But because love, to them, means availability.

A man will say yes when he should say no.

Yes to extra work.
Yes to more responsibility.
Yes to expectations that stretch him beyond his limits.

Because he believes that saying no might mean letting someone down.

And letting someone down hurts him more than hurting himself

It means showing up even when they are empty.

A man will say yes when he should say no.

Yes to extra work.
Yes to more responsibility.
Yes to expectations that stretch him beyond his limits.

Because he believes that saying no might mean letting someone down.

And letting someone down hurts him more than hurting himself.

Money becomes another silent battlefield.

A man feels pressure even before the wallet opens.

He worries:

If I ask my wife for money, what will she think?
Will she feel I am incapable?
Will she doubt me?

So he doesn't ask.

He adjusts.

He borrows quietly.
He delays his own needs.
He sacrifices silently.

He doesn't do this because his wife wouldn't help.

He does it because his pride is tangled with responsibility.

Because he was taught that a man should manage—
no matter the cost.

Inside him, questions never stop.

Am I enough?
Am I doing enough?
What if I fail them?

And yet, outwardly, he looks calm.

This chapter is not here to create anger.

It is here to create understanding.

Men are not hiding emotions to be distant.

They are hiding them to protect the people they love.

If you're a woman reading this, pause.

The man in your life may not say he is tired—but he feels it.
He may not say he is scared—but he carries it.
He may not ask for support—but he needs it.

Not because he is weak.

Because he is human.

If you're a man reading this and feeling exposed, breathe.

You are not broken for feeling this way.

You are not less of a man for needing rest.

You are not incapable for needing help.

This book is not blaming anyone.

It is giving words to emotions that were never taught how to speak.

If your eyes are heavy right now, let them be.

These tears are not sadness.

They are recognition

Every man deserves a space where he can say:

"I am tired."
"I am scared."
"I need support too."

And still be respected.

And still be loved.

And still be enough.

This chapter was written for the sentences that never made it out of your mouth.

But lived in your heart every single day.

You are seen.

And you are not alone.

If Only Someone Had Asked, "Are You Okay?"

Sometimes, a man doesn't need advice.

He doesn't need solutions.
He doesn't need motivation.

He just needs one simple question.

"Are you okay?"

Not asked casually.
Not asked in passing.

Asked with patience.
Asked with genuine concern.

Most days, no one asks.

They assume.

They assume he's strong.
They assume he can handle it.
They assume silence means stability.

And he lets them assume.

Because correcting them feels harder than enduring.

He has become good at carrying things alone.

So good that people forget he is carrying anything at all.

If someone had asked him that question at the right time…

He might have paused.

He might have exhaled.
He might have said something real.

But time passed.

Responsibilities grew.

And the question never came.

He learns to live without being asked.

To self-soothe.
To self-motivate.
To self-survive.

But even the strongest systems need maintenance.

There are moments when he hopes someone notices.

The slower steps.
The distant eyes.
The forced smile.

But no one does.

Not because they don't care.

Because they are busy surviving too.

This is how emotional distance is born.

Not from cruelty.

From unawareness.

If you are a partner reading this, remember:

Asking “Are you okay?” doesn’t weaken a man.

It gives him permission.

Permission to be honest.
Permission to be human.

If you are a man reading this, remember:

You don’t have to wait to be asked.

You are allowed to speak.

This chapter isn’t about blame.

It’s about bridges.

Bridges between silence and support.

One question can change a day.

One conversation can change a life.

And if no one has asked you yet…

Let this book ask you now.

Are you okay?

And if the answer is no…

That’s okay too.

He Loved Quietly, and the World Missed It

Some love makes noise.

It announces itself.
It demands recognition.
It wants to be seen and celebrated.

A man's love is often different.

It is quiet.

So quiet that the world misses it.

He doesn't always say "I love you."

He shows it by staying.
By working late.
By choosing responsibility when escape would be easier.

He shows it by fixing what's broken, even when he himself feels broken.

When the family sleeps peacefully, he feels successful.

When bills are paid on time, he feels proud.

When his wife smiles, even briefly, his tiredness feels worth it.

This is how he loves.

But quiet love is risky.

Because what is not spoken is often not noticed.

People notice flowers.
They notice sweet messages.
They notice grand gestures.

They don't notice a man skipping his own needs so others can have more.

They don't notice the pressure he carries in his chest every day.

Sometimes, he wonders if his love even counts.

Not because he doubts his feelings.

But because no one seems to recognize them.

He hears words like:

"He doesn't express."
"He's emotionally unavailable."
"He doesn't care like before."

And he stays silent.

Because explaining himself feels like begging to be understood.

But silence doesn't mean absence.

It means he trusted his actions to speak for him.

This chapter is for every man whose love went unnoticed.

For every man who loved deeply but quietly

If you are a partner reading this, pause.

That man beside you may not say much.

But look closely.

Look at what he gives up.
Look at what he prioritizes.
Look at how he shows up even when he's exhausted.

That is love.

If you are a man reading this and feeling unseen, know this:

Your love mattered.
Your effort counted.
Even if no one clapped.

Love doesn't always need applause.

Sometimes, it just needs acknowledgment.

This book is doing that now.

It is saying what the world forgot to say.

"I see you."

And sometimes, being seen is enough to keep going.

The Day He Felt Seen

It didn't happen with applause.

There was no dramatic speech.
No grand apology.
No sudden transformation.

It happened quietly.

The way most important things do.

It was an ordinary evening.

The kind he had lived a thousand times before.

Work done.
Dinner finished.

TV playing in the background.

Nothing special.

He was sitting there, tired in a way he had stopped explaining years ago.

His wife looked at him.

Not glanced.

Looked.

As if she was finally seeing him… not as a role, but as a person.

She said softly,
"You've been carrying a lot, haven't you?"

That was it.

One sentence.

No accusations.
No complaints.
No demands.

Just recognition.

Something inside him loosened.

Not completely.

But enough to breathe.

He didn't answer immediately.

Because when a man is finally seen, words don't rush out.

They hesitate.

They are afraid this moment might disappear.

He nodded.

Just once.

She didn't interrupt.

Didn't correct.

Didn't explain herself.

She sat beside him.

Close enough to say, you're not alone, without saying anything at all.

In that silence, years of weight shifted.

Not gone.

Just shared.

For the first time in a long time, he didn't feel like he had to perform strength.

He didn't feel like he had to explain his silence.

He didn't feel misunderstood.

That night, he slept differently.

Not longer.

Deeper.

Being seen doesn't erase problems.

It doesn't pay loans.
It doesn't remove responsibility.
It doesn't magically heal exhaustion.

But it changes something fundamental.

It reminds a man that he exists beyond duty.

Many men don't need solutions.

They need acknowledgment.

They need to know that their effort is visible.

That their silence was noticed.

That their love was understood.

If you are a woman reading this, remember:

Sometimes your man isn't distant.

He's tired of explaining.

Seeing him—really seeing him—can do more than a hundred arguments.

If you are a man reading this and hoping for that moment, hear this:

You deserve to be seen.

Not just as a provider.
Not just as a protector.

As a human being.

This chapter isn't a fantasy.

It's a reminder.

Understanding doesn't require perfection.

It requires presence.

And when a man finally feels seen…

He doesn't become weaker.

He becomes lighter.

Hope, Slowly Returning

Hope doesn't rush back.

It doesn't knock loudly or announce itself.

It returns the way morning light enters a dark room—
slowly, gently, almost unnoticed at first.

After being seen, something inside a man softens.

He still wakes up with responsibilities.
Still carries pressure.
Still worries about the future.

But the weight no longer sits alone on his chest.

It is shared now.

And sharing changes everything.

He starts speaking again.

Not long speeches.
Not emotional outbursts.

Small sentences.

"Today was hard."
"I'm worried about this."
"I don't know how to handle that."

Each sentence feels risky.

But each one lands safely.

Hope grows from safety.

From knowing you won't be judged.
From knowing your honesty won't be used against you later.
From knowing silence is no longer your only option.

He notices changes.

He laughs without forcing it.
He listens without zoning out.
He comes home less tense.

Not because life became easier—
but because he doesn't feel alone inside it anymore.

His wife changes too.

She listens differently.
She asks more gently.
She complains less harshly.

Not because she stopped feeling hurt—
but because she understands where his silence came from.

Understanding doesn't erase differences.

It creates patience.

There are still arguments.

Still misunderstandings.

Still days when words fail.

But now, there is repair.

Now, there is effort from both sides.

Hope teaches a man something important.

He doesn't have to be perfect to be loved.

He doesn't have to carry everything silently to be respected.

Slowly, he allows himself small dreams again.

Not big, risky ones.

Simple ones.

Peaceful evenings.
Honest conversations.
A home that feels safe emotionally, not just physically.

If you're reading this and feeling a little warmth inside, hold onto it.

That warmth is hope.

And hope doesn't mean everything will be okay.

It means you're no longer giving up on yourself.

This chapter is not about happy endings.

It's about beginnings of healing.

A man doesn't need the world to change.

He needs one place where he doesn't have to wear armor.

And when he finds that place…

He starts living again.

Not just surviving.

Love After Silence

Silence changes people.

Not because silence is cruel,
but because it leaves too much unsaid.

For years, love existed in actions, not words.
In duty, not expression.
In sacrifice, not sharing.

And both of you survived that silence.

But survival is not the same as living.

When silence finally breaks, love doesn't rush back like it used to.

It walks slowly.

Carefully.

As if afraid of being misunderstood again.

You notice it in small things.

The way conversations pause before becoming arguments.
The way apologies come sooner than pride.
The way listening matters more than winning.

Love after silence is mature.

It knows pain.
It respects boundaries.

It chooses kindness deliberately.

You no longer assume.

You ask.

You no longer hide.
You explain.
You no longer expect perfection.

You expect effort.

There are moments when old habits try to return.

You feel the urge to stay quiet again.
She feels the urge to complain instead of asking.

But now, awareness steps in.

And awareness changes reactions.

You learn something important.

Love isn't about who suffered more.

It's about who is willing to understand more.

Forgiveness becomes quieter too.

No dramatic statements.
No emotional scenes.

Just a choice made every day.

I will not punish you for what you didn't know then.

You still have scars.

Both of you do.

But scars don't mean damage.

They mean healing happened.

If you are reading this and thinking about your own relationship, pause.

Ask yourself:

Have we spoken enough about what hurt us?
Have we listened without preparing a defense?
Have we allowed each other to change?

Love after silence is not fragile.

It is careful.

And careful love lasts longer.

This chapter is for those who didn't give up on each other—
even when words were missing for years.

When Quiet Love Finally Gets Understood

Understanding does not arrive with noise.

It arrives softly.

Almost late.
Almost shy.

It comes after exhaustion.
After tears that no one saw.
After fights that were never really about the fight.

It comes when both of you are tired of hurting each other.

Quiet love was always there.

It just didn't know how to speak.

He loved in responsibility.
In waking up every day even when he didn't want to.
In carrying pressure silently so no one else had to.

She loved in waiting.
In hoping he would notice without being told.
In believing that one day he would feel what she was feeling.

Both were loving.
Both were lonely.

The misunderstanding was never about love.

It was about language.

One night, nothing dramatic happens.

No argument.
No tears.
No accusations.

Just a moment.

He sits there longer than usual.
She doesn't rush away like before.

Silence returns—but this time, it feels different.

Not heavy.
Not sharp.

Just honest.

"I didn't know you felt this alone," she says quietly.

And for the first time, he doesn't joke.
Doesn't deflect.
Doesn't stay strong.

He exhales.

"I didn't know how to say it," he replies.

That's it.

That's the moment.

Not a big speech.
Not a breakdown.

Just truth, spoken without armour

Understanding doesn't fix everything instantly.

But it softens everything.

She starts noticing things she once ignored.

The way he checks his phone late at night, calculating numbers.
The way he says "it's fine" even when it isn't.
The way he never buys anything for himself.

He starts noticing her silence.

Not the peaceful one.
The hurting one.

The silence that says, I need you, but I'm tired of asking.

Rebuilding intimacy doesn't begin in the bedroom.

It begins in safety.

In knowing that speaking won't start a war.
In trusting that honesty won't be used as a weapon.

He starts sharing small things first.

A worry about money.
A fear about the future.
A moment of doubt.

She listens.

Not to respond.
Not to correct.

Just to understand.

She starts asking gently.

Not accusing.

Not comparing.

Just asking.

"How are you really?"
"What are you carrying today?"
"Where can I stand with you?"

Healing together is slow.

There are days when old wounds reopen.
When habits fight back.
When silence almost returns.

But now, there is a pause before the silence.

And in that pause, one of them reaches out.

Quiet love, when understood, becomes powerful.

Because it doesn't need to prove itself anymore.

It just is.

He no longer feels invisible.

She no longer feels alone.

They don't love louder.

They love clearer.

If you are reading this and feeling tears in your eyes,
it's because this isn't just their story.

It's yours.

The love you gave but couldn't explain.
The love you needed but didn't know how to ask for.

The love that stayed—even when misunderstood.

Quiet love doesn't disappear.

It waits.

And when it is finally understood,
it doesn't shout.

It holds you.

And says,
"I was here all along."

When Love Learns to Speak and Stay

Love doesn't fail because people stop loving.

Love struggles because people stop feeling safe enough to speak.

This chapter is about that safety.
The kind that doesn't shout.
The kind that doesn't judge.
The kind that stays—even when the truth is uncomfortable.

Learning to Speak Needs Without Fear

For the longest time, you believed silence was strength.

You thought, If I don't say it, it won't hurt anyone.
You thought, If I manage it alone, I'm being responsible.

But silence has a cost.

It doesn't disappear.
It settles inside you.

It becomes tiredness, distance, anger, and eventually misunderstanding.

Speaking needs feels risky.

What if they don't understand?
What if they think I'm weak?
What if they think I'm complaining?

So you stay quiet.

And she waits.

And both of you suffer differently.

The truth is simple, but hard to accept:

Unspoken needs turn into unintentional wounds.

Learning to speak doesn't mean blaming.

It means sharing.

Instead of saying,
"You never understand me,"
you learn to say,
"I need you to listen without correcting me."

Instead of saying,
"You don't care,"
you say,
"I feel alone when I carry this by myself."

This is not weakness.

This is courage.

When a man speaks his needs, he isn't losing respect.

He is building trust.

And when a woman speaks her needs, she isn't demanding.

She is inviting connection.

How Emotional Safety Changes Marriage

Emotional safety is not about agreement.

It's about permission.

Permission to be tired.
Permission to be scared.
Permission to say, I don't know what I'm doing.

In emotionally safe marriages, arguments don't disappear.

But fear does.

You're no longer scared of being misunderstood forever.
You're no longer scared that honesty will be used against you.

You know this:

Even if we fight, we are still on the same side.

Emotional safety changes everything.

Silence becomes a pause, not a wall.
Disagreements become conversations, not threats.
Mistakes become lessons, not weapons.

You stop walking on eggshells.

You start walking together.

She feels safer expressing her pain without being labeled emotional.
He feels safer admitting pressure without being called weak.

This safety doesn't come automatically.

It is built.

Slowly.

Through consistent kindness.
Through listening without interrupting.
Through choosing understanding over ego.

How Love Matures After Pain

Young love wants perfection.

Mature love wants peace.

Pain teaches love important lessons.

It teaches patience.
It teaches humility.
It teaches forgiveness without forgetting.

After pain, love stops demanding and starts accepting.

Not settling.
Understanding.

You no longer expect your partner to fill every gap.

You learn to support each other instead of completing each other.

You stop asking,
"Why are you like this?"

And start asking,
"What made you like this?"

This is where tolerance is born.

Not forced tolerance.

Human tolerance.

The kind that says,
You're not perfect, and neither am I.

And we still choose each other.

Building a Never-Breakable Relationship

Unbreakable doesn't mean unshakable.

It means repairable.

A strong marriage is not one without cracks.

It's one where cracks are fixed with care.

Love holds the relationship together.
Tolerance prevents unnecessary damage.
Patience allows growth.
Understanding keeps both hearts soft.

You stop keeping score.

You stop competing over sacrifices.

You start appreciating effort instead of demanding results.

On hard days, you remember:

We are tired, not enemies.
We are learning, not failing.
We are growing, not drifting.

You speak even when your voice shakes.
You listen even when it's uncomfortable.
You stay even when walking away seems easier.

That is lifelong love.

This chapter is not advice.It is a mirror.

If you see yourself here,
it means your love is not broken.

It is becoming wiser.

Epilogue: To the Man Who Kept Going

If you have reached here, this book was never just a book for you.

It was a mirror.
It was a quiet conversation.
It was someone finally sitting beside you and saying,
"I see you."

You didn't read these pages.
You lived them.

In the tired mornings.
In the long nights.
In the responsibilities that came without training.
In the love you gave without announcing.

You were never weak.

You were just carrying too much without being taught how to put it down.

You became a husband, a son, a provider, a protector—
sometimes all in one day—
without a pause, without applause, without preparation.

And still, you showed up.

You learned that love after marriage is not about romance alone.

It is about staying.
About choosing patience when anger feels easier.
About choosing understanding when silence feels safer.

It is about loving people in different ways, at the same time,
and feeling guilty no matter what you do.

There were moments when you felt invisible.

When your sacrifices were assumed, not appreciated.
When your strength was expected, not supported.
When your silence was misunderstood as distance.

Yet you stayed.

This book did not blame.

It listened.

It did not accuse.

It understood.

Because this story was never about men versus women,
or wife versus parents.

It was about humans trying to love without losing themselves.

If you are a man reading this, know this:

You are allowed to be tired.
You are allowed to feel scared.
You are allowed to need support too.

Speaking does not make you less of a man.
Feeling does not make you weak.

It makes you human.

If you are a woman reading this, know this:

Your sacrifices are real.
Your pain is valid.
Your love is powerful.

And when both sides are seen,
marriage stops being a battlefield
and becomes a partnership again.

The purpose of this book was not to create anger.

It was to create understanding.

To remind you that love does not disappear after marriage.

It evolves.

If this book made you cry, pause, or reflect,
then it has done its job.

Not because it was well written,
but because it was already written inside you.

Carry this truth forward:

A strong marriage is not built by perfect people.
It is built by honest ones.

People who talk even when it's hard.
Who listen even when it hurts.
Who stay even when it's heavy.

And if one day you feel lost again,
remember this:

You were never alone in your silence.

This book was proof.

You kept going.
And that matters more than you know.

He wakes up.

He works.

He adjusts.

He smiles.

Not because life is easy.

But because quitting was never taught to him.

That is a man after marriage.

ABOUT THE AUTHOR

Rakesh Singh is the author of the widely appreciated book *Under The Table* and a passionate writer whose love for storytelling began during his school days at **Kendriya Vidyalaya, IIT Kharagpur, West Bengal**.

Professionally, Rakesh is a **Microsoft Certified AI Data Engineer**, a **Microsoft Copilot Expert**, and a **Python-certified professional from IIT Madras**. He has also been part of multiple **AI tools and technology workshops at IIT Delhi**, combining strong technical expertise with a deep understanding of human behavior. His work reflects a rare balance between logic and emotion—data and heart.

Writing, however, has always been more than a skill for him—it is a calling. From winning writing competitions during school to being recognized within and outside the organizations he has worked with, Rakesh has consistently used words to express what many feel but cannot say.

Currently residing in **Gurugram, Haryana**, Rakesh brings to life the untold emotional journey of men after marriage. Through this book, he highlights a reality faced by men across the world—the silent struggle of balancing love, family, responsibility, and work, often without recognition and without complaint.

Man After Marriage is deeply personal. It carries Rakesh's own experiences—the confusion, the pressure, the emotional silence—shared not as a complaint, but as understanding. This book does not speak *for* men; it speaks *from* within them. Every page is a mirror, reflecting emotions that many husbands, sons, and fathers quietly carry inside.

At the same time, the book respects and acknowledges women—their sacrifices, strength, and emotional journey—making it a bridge of understanding rather than division.

With clarity of thought, emotional depth, and gentle honesty, Rakesh Singh gives words to feelings that usually remain unspoken. His writing does not demand attention—it earns it. And in doing so, he gives every reader, man or woman, the comfort of being seen, heard, and understood.

www.ingramcontent.com/pod-product-compliance
Ingram Content Group UK Ltd.
Pitfield, Milton Keynes, MK11 3LW, UK
UKHW041318190726
13845UKWH00025B/349

9 789356 357808